LIVING TOGETHER

Is Marriage the Better Buy?

**Richard Collins &
Tanya Roberts**

Acknowledgements

The publisher and authors owe a debt of gratitude to Conrad Dehn QC who conceived the idea of this book and who, with Maryly La Follette and Clare Renton, made available a first draft.

The authors are also very grateful to many people who have most generously helped in the writing of this book. Among those who were particularly helpful at Charles Russell are Andrew Cameron, Julia Staines, David Green, Caroline Clark, Rachel Wookey, Sarah Whitten, Emma Vardy, Sarah Anticoni, Sarah Higgins, Gabriella Wright, Lande Belo, Louise Clark, Anna Mortlock, Robin Bynoe, Philippa Glynn, Beverley Thompson and Sandra Badger.

Special thanks also go to Deepak Nagpal at 1 King's Bench Walk, Jeff Roberts of Collins Benson Goldhill, David Long of Osbornes Solicitors and Kate Pasfield of the CAB at the Principal Registry.

Living Together
© 2004 Lawpack Publishing Limited

Lawpack Publishing Limited
76-89 Alscot Road
London SE1 3AW
www.lawpack.co.uk

Printed in Great Britain
ISBN: 1 902646 26 6
All rights reserved.

About the authors

Richard Collins is a solicitor at Charles Russell Solicitors in London. He is a mature entrant to family law, having first worked in advertising for Saatchi & Saatchi and other agencies. He has extensive experience of dealing with the financial consequences of the breakdown of relationships, often with an international element, and cases involving disputes about children, cohabitation issues, pre-nuptial agreements and issues relating to the unmarried family. He has made regular appearances in print and broadcast media. He is married with two children.

Tanya Roberts is also a solicitor at Charles Russell Solicitors. She graduated from Leeds University and joined Charles Russell in 1992. Her practice includes financial and children-related cases, both domestic and international. She is on the Lord Chancellor's Panel of Solicitors for child abduction work and has, with two others, written a book on the subject called *International Child Abduction*. She is married with two daughters.

Contents

Introduction

For most men and women who want to move in together or who are already living together, a key question is, 'Should we get married?' To some the answer is clear: they consider marriage to be an institution sanctified by religion or they prefer to make a formal commitment to the person they love regardless of the practical consequences. We do not dispute the validity or importance of either of these approaches but there are still many couples who are happy to live together, married or not.

There are estimated to be 1,800,000 couples in Great Britain living together outside marriage at the moment who need to consider the practical consequences when deciding whether to marry. Under English law, marriage changes people's rights and obligations drastically. In some areas of the law, the recent tendency has been for Parliament to equate the position of those who live together unmarried in the same household, acting as husband and wife, to those who are married, but important differences still remain.

There are also existing arguments over whether an unmarried couple are living 'in the same household' and 'as husband and wife'. The Department of Social Security (DSS) attach importance to whether:

(a) the man is normally living in the same household as the woman and has no other home;

(b) they are living together in a stable 'marital-like' relationship – signs of which may include children of the union, the woman using the man's name and a joint lifestyle;

(c) there is some mutual financial support or sharing of household expenses;

(d) there is some sort of sexual relationship (although this is not essential);

(e) they are caring for a child of the union;

(f) they act publicly as man and wife (although use of the same surname is not essential). The courts have also said that for a couple to be living together as man and wife it is necessary that they should have a settled intention to be so regarded.

Professional experience has taught us that the legal effects of marriage often take people by surprise. As a result, when contemplating marriage, couples should know what the changes are.

One of the most important issues is that marriage affects your right to support from the other person, as well as your ability to retain your own income and property, or to receive some of the other person's when you break up. In particular, marriage dramatically affects your right to your partner's property after a break-up or death.

Major areas where your legal position will be changed by marriage include those concerning your children, home, tax and social security plus there are other, lesser known areas that can be affected, such as crime and life assurance. This book aims to deal with them all.

Living Together only deals with the general law affecting everybody and not with private contractual arrangements. Private pension schemes, for example, often provide pensions for employees' widows or widowers but not for their unmarried partners. Therefore, if your partner belongs to such a pension scheme, this may be an argument in favour of marriage. However, this topic is outside the scope of this book so we recommend that you research this yourself or take advice.

The law is changing all the time with new bills continually being introduced, for example, the Government is presently planning to introduce a domestic violence, crime and victims bill. As a result, we can only guarantee that this book is accurate at the time of going to press. We summarise English & Welsh law as at 1 May 2004 (and the post March 2004 Budget figures are included).

Definitions

- In this book the word 'partner' is used to describe the person of the opposite sex with whom you live in one household as husband and wife but to whom you are not married.

- For convenience (and for no other reason), 'him', 'he' and 'his' have been used throughout and should be read to include 'her', 'she' and 'her'.

Chapter 1

Is marriage an option?

Marriage

Single

- If you are single you can marry anyone except:

  (a) someone married; **or**

  (b) someone with whom you are not allowed to have sexual intercourse (see page 12); **or**

  (c) your uncle, aunt, nephew or niece.

- So, for example, a man can lawfully have his niece, aged over 16, as his partner but he cannot marry her.

- To marry someone under the age of 18 you require the consent of any parent with parental responsibility or the leave of the court.

- You cannot marry:

  (a) your stepdaughter or stepson;

  (b) your stepfather or stepmother;

  (c) your stepgrandparent; **or**

  (d) your stepgrandchild; **if**

    (i) either of you are under 21; **or**

    (ii) the younger of you has, before the age of 18, been treated as a child of the other's family;

  and you cannot marry:

(e) your ex-mother-in-law or ex-father-in-law; **or**

(f) your ex-son-in-law or ex-daughter-in-law; **if**

(i) either of you are under 21; **or**

(ii) either of your ex-spouses are still alive or the other parent of that spouse is still alive.

Married

- If you are married you cannot marry anyone else.

Sexual intercourse

Unmarried

- You may have sexual intercourse with anyone of the opposite sex over the age of 16 except your grandparent, parent, brother, sister, child or grandchild. It is a crime if you have sex with any of these people and you risk prosecution. If you are married, your spouse will also have grounds for divorcing you, with serious consequences.

Married

- If you have sex with anyone of the opposite sex apart from your spouse, you will be guilty of adultery. Your spouse can, if he finds it intolerable, divorce you with serious consequences unless he lives with you as husband and wife for six months after finding out about your last act of adultery.

- If you have sex with anyone who is under 16 or your grandparent, parent, brother, sister, or half-brother or half-sister, child or grandchild, you are guilty of a crime and risk prosecution.

Chapter 2
What about children?

Subject to the court's power to regulate its exercise and subject to the rights of the other parent, 'parental responsibility' includes the following obligations and rights:

- To maintain the child until the age of 18 or until he ceases full-time education.

- To protect the child.

- To discipline the child.

- To determine the child's education.

- To decide where the child will live up to the age of 16.

- To consent to medical treatment for the child up to the age of 16.

- To ensure the child receives suitable full-time education – a breach of which may lead to criminal prosecution.

- To consent to the child's marriage under the age of 18.

- To choose the child's name or religion.

- To take the child abroad.

Non-financial responsibility

Unmarried

While you are living together

- A mother has parental responsibility for her child, which can come to an end only on:

    (a) the death of the child, the child's adoption or the child attaining the age of 18; **or**

    (b) her death.

- The father of a child does not have parental responsibility for the child unless he:

    (a) enters into a parental responsibility agreement with the mother in the prescribed form; **or**

    (b) obtains an order of the court; **or**

    (c) marries the mother; **or**

    (d) acquires it automatically by being on the birth certificate (only applies to fathers of children born after 1 December 2003).

- When the court is deciding whether to make a parental responsibility order in favour of the father, it will treat the child's welfare as paramount. It must be satisfied that making the order is better for the child than making no order at all. Factors the court may take into account include:

    (a) the commitment the father has shown towards the child;

    (b) the degree of attachment that exists between the father and the child; **and**

    (c) the reasons why the father is applying for the order.

- Even if the father obtains a parental responsibility order or makes such an agreement with the mother, this can be terminated by a later court order and this order can be applied for by anyone with parental responsibility or even by the child himself.

- Even if the father does not have parental responsibility for the child, he has, like a married father, a right to apply to the court for any type of order relating to the child. The orders he can apply for are for:

    (a) residence (which would give him parental responsibility);

    (b) contact;

    (c) one to prohibit particular steps being taken; **and**

    (d) one to determine any particular issue that has arisen.

- Unless the father has parental responsibility, the mother can take the child abroad without the father's consent. If the mother takes the child abroad and the father has parental responsibility, he can make an application under the Hague Convention for the child's return (unless one of the limited defences apply, e.g. acquiescence or there is a grave risk of physical or psychological harm if the child is returned). He may also be able to rely on the European Convention if he has a 'custody' order or he can enforce an order giving him 'access'. (Please see the Appendix for a list of countries in which the Hague and European Conventions are in force.)

- If there is disagreement over who is the father of the child, the court can order blood tests to be taken. The court takes the general view that it is preferable for the biological parentage of a child to be known. If the mother is married to someone else, her husband will be presumed to be the father unless the contrary is proved.

- A father can seek a declaration of paternity. If he succeeds, he can require the Register of Births to be amended to state that he is the father.

- If the mother has the child by artificial insemination by a donor other than her partner, even with her partner's consent, the partner will not be treated as the child's father unless the insemination was in the course of treatment provided for them both by someone officially licensed.

If you cease living together

- Unless the court has made an order that the father has parental responsibility or the parents have made a parental responsibility agreement in the prescribed form, only the mother has parental responsibility for the child (unless the child is born after 1 December 2003 and the father is on the birth certificate, then he has parental responsibility automatically – see page 16).

- If there is a dispute as to the child's upbringing, including such matters as his name or taking him abroad, the court will decide in the child's best interests. If the father has no parental responsibility, he will have to make an application before the court will stop the mother from making a unilateral decision.

- If the father wishes the child to live with him and the mother objects, he will have to obtain a residence order from the court.

- If the father has not got parental responsibility, the court will only make a residence order if it also makes a parental responsibility order.

Conclusion

- The unmarried father who has parental responsibility is in a stronger position than one who has not. On the other hand, if the father only wants to retain contact with the child, he can seek a contact order from the court without having parental responsibility. A contact order will enable him to see the child or have the child stay as often as the court sees fit.

- If your partner has a child by a former partner and you form a close relationship with the child, you need the leave of the court before you can apply for the child to live with you or to enable you to keep contact with him, unless you have lived with the child for three years immediately before your application.

Married

While you are living together

- Parental responsibility rests with you both equally. Each of you has equal and separate obligations and rights. If there is a dispute between you as to the exercise of any of these obligations or rights, the court can decide.

- Any child born during the marriage will be presumed to be the child of the mother and her husband. If it is disputed that he is the father, the court may order blood tests to be taken.

- If a child has been carried by a woman as a result of artificial insemination, and the sperm used was not her husband's, he will be treated as the father of the child unless he did not consent to the procedure.

If you have been married

- You both retain parental responsibility for any child.

- If you cannot agree on any issue, you can ask the court to adjudicate.

- Neither of you can remove the child from the country without the other's consent or a court order unless one of you has a residence order. Then you may take the child out of the country for up to one month without the other parent's consent.

- If you have a stepchild, you can, when your marriage comes to an end, without prior leave of the court, apply to the court for the child to live with you or for an order to enable you to keep contact with the child.

Conclusion

- If you marry, you will acquire parental responsibility automatically. It is only unmarried fathers of children born after 1 December 2003 who acquire it automatically if they are on the birth certificate.

> • It is easier for a step-parent than it is for a partner to obtain an order enabling him to continue to play a part in someone else's child's life after the relationship with the child's parent has ended.

Financial responsibility

Unmarried

- Both the father and the mother are under an obligation to maintain their child. Before a man can be compelled to do so, he must admit or have been proved to be the child's father. The parent not living with the child will have to maintain the child and the amount will be assessed by the Child Support Agency (CSA). Alternatively, the parents can agree themselves to maintenance in a court order.

- The court does not ordinarily have the jurisdiction to make an order for maintenance (called 'periodical payments') between the parents unless the order is agreed by both parties or there is a pre-existing order in force. An order for payments above the CSA limit can be made if the non-resident parent's net income (after pension) is £104,000 per year or more.

- The court can, however, make orders for the payment of a lump sum or transfer of property for the benefit of the child, although these orders are not usually used beyond the extent necessary to maintain or house the child until the child reaches the age of 18 or ceases full-time education.

- The court order will depend upon:

  (a) the income, earning capacity and financial resources which each parent has, or is likely to have, in the foreseeable future;

  (b) the financial needs and obligations which each parent has, or is likely to have, in the foreseeable future;

  (c) the financial needs of the child;

  (d) the income, earning capacity (if any) and financial resources of the child;

  (e) any physical or mental disability of the child;

  (f) the manner in which the child is being, or expected to be, educated or trained.

- If your partner has a child of whom you are not the parent:

  (a) you are under no obligation to maintain the child;

  (b) you do not have to support your partner even though he is, for example, prevented from working by the need to stay at home and care for the child.

Married

- Both parents are under an obligation to maintain their child.

- The court has the same power as it has where the parents are unmarried to make an order against the non-resident parent for periodical payments above the CSA limit (£104,000), or the payment of a lump sum or transfer of property for the benefit of the child. However, a spouse does have spousal claims for maintenance, a lump sum, a transfer of property and a share of a pension.

- If your spouse has a child by a former partner or spouse and you treat that stepchild as a child of the family, the court has the same power to order you to maintain him as if he were your own if the natural parent cannot provide. This wouldn't be via the CSA but via the court process. The amount the court will order you to pay will depend, amongst other things, on your circumstances and on:

  (a) whether, and if so to what extent, for how long and on what basis you have supported the child;

  (b) whether at the time you gave your support you knew the child was not yours;

  (c) who else has a duty to maintain the child.

If, for example, you have supported your stepchild for most of his life and the father is nowhere to be found, you may have to go on paying until the child is grown up.

Conclusion

- Marriage affects your obligations towards stepchildren.

Adoption

Unmarried

- You cannot adopt a child jointly. One can adopt and then a residence order can be granted to both.

- The father's consent is not necessary for the child's adoption, unless he has acquired parental or custodial rights. However, he should be informed.

Married

- The court will only allow one of you to adopt a child without the other if:

    (a) your spouse cannot be found; **or**

    (b) you are living apart in such circumstances that the separation is likely to be permanent; **or**

    (c) your spouse is incapable of making an application for an adoption order.

Conclusion

- Wanting to adopt a child jointly with your partner is an argument in favour of marriage.

The child's position

Unmarried

- The child's rights will be no less than if his parents were married, except in three respects:

  (a) Nationality and immigration – see page 93.

  (b) Inheritance of titles – see page 101.

  (c) The child may be unable to find out who his father is if his mother does not tell him and his father's name does not appear on the birth certificate. This may lead (apart from insecurity and unhappiness) to the child being deprived of the opportunity of inheriting on his father's death. Whether the child has a legal right to compel his mother to disclose the name or to sue her for damages for breach of duty leading to this loss of opportunity has not yet been tested in English & Welsh law.

- The child may seek a declaration of parentage. This may enable him to inherit on his father's intestacy or, if dependent on his father, make an application to the court for provision from his father's estate if he left a Will (see page 78).

Married

- If the parents are married, there is a presumption of legitimacy and unless there is evidence to the contrary, the husband of the mother of the child will be presumed to be the father.

Chapter 3
Will you be safe in your home?

Ownership of the home

Ownership of the home is an important issue if you are living together unmarried. It is not such a problem, however, if you are married, unless death or bankruptcy occurs (see page 34 for further information).

When you are married, the court has the discretion to adjust property rights between you depending on various factors including the means and needs of each of you – the first consideration being the welfare of any children.

Unmarried

- Ownership will depend on:

    (a) who is the legal owner of the home (i.e. whose name appears on the title deeds, Land Registry documentation, lease or rent book); and

    (b) any agreement, oral or in writing, under which the legal owner and his partner agreed to share the ownership. Initially, the court has to decide whether you and your partner agreed that the home was to be shared before the purchase.

    If the answer is 'Yes', the court then has to conclude whether the one whose name is not on the title deeds relied to his disadvantage on this arrangement and the court will examine the course of dealing between you. If you did act to your disadvantage, the court will decide that the property is beneficially owned by you both.

If the answer is 'No', the court has to decide if an arrangement, understanding or intention that the property was to be shared can be seen from your past course of dealing with each other.

If the court concludes that it was intended for the partner whose name is not on the title deeds to have a share, the court will then decide what proportion each party will receive. This will depend on the parties' joint intention or on their contributions. The court often decides that the shares should be equal, but this decision will vary depending on the facts in every case. The share will be valued at the date of sale of the property or at the date of trial.

• The mere fact that you have lived in your partner's home for a long time, provide household services and bring up your joint children there together, will not make you a part owner of the property or establish an arrangement or common intention that you should be. Ordinary principles of law apply and the court cannot vary the rights of the parties, even in what may appear the most deserving of cases, for example, if you have been engaged to be married and your partner has broken off the engagement. The only exception to this instance is if, during your engagement, one of you has substantially improved the property of the other. He will therefore be entitled to a share or a bigger share in it.

- If you provide part of the purchase price or mortgage instalments, or pay for repairs or improvements with the owner's consent, then, even if there was no express agreement between you about it, the court may decide that this is evidence of an agreement or common intention that you should have a share or possibly that your partner holds the property partly for your benefit, which will have much the same effect. Many attempts to prove such arrangements in court fail. Contributing towards household expenses is generally not enough. However, this may show that you both intended to have an interest in the property if by contributing to the expenses, you have enabled your partner to pay the mortgage, etc out of funds that he would otherwise be forced to spend on housekeeping.

- If your partner is the owner or tenant of the home, and you have a child by him and the relationship breaks down, you can apply to the court to have the property or tenancy transferred either to you for the child or to the child himself, but on the basis that the property reverts to the payer once the child attains independence. Whether the court will do so depends on the facts. The court does not have the power to enforce such an order if your partner is not the child's parent.

- If the home is in joint names and was purchased as a family home, the court may stop one of the two joint owners from selling the property until it is no longer needed for a family home. If there are children, this may force one parent to wait many years until he can recover his share. However, even where there are no children, one of you may have to wait until the other can move to suitable accommodation before the house can be sold.

Married

- Marriage itself gives neither spouse legal rights of ownership (as opposed to occupation) that they did not have before. However, the court has the power to adjust property ownership on divorce. Furthermore, you have better claims as a spouse against your spouse's estate on his death.

- If you contribute substantially to the value of the home, you will be treated as having acquired a share, or a larger share, in it accordingly. However, this does not necessarily mean that you will end up with a greater share as the court takes a whole range of factors into account when deciding on how ownership of the home will be divided (see page 73).

- If you had agreed that you would pay for food and housekeeping out of your earnings so that your spouse could make the mortgage repayments out of his, the court will more readily infer a joint venture in which each was intended to participate and therefore both of you will have a share in the home.

- On divorce, the court can and will vary your legal rights. The owner of the home may have to transfer the whole of it to the other spouse for nothing. The court gives priority to the welfare of any children under the age of 18 and the need of both husband and wife to have a roof over their heads.

Conclusion

- If you are married, you can gain property rights you did not have before marriage and you can lose property rights you did have before marriage. The married homeowner risks losing his home on divorce while marriage gives the non-owner security he would not otherwise have had.

Occupation of the home

Unmarried

- Your right to remain in the home or to evict your partner will be determined by your respective legal interests in the home and by any agreement made between you or any permission either of you may have granted to the other.

- If the home or tenancy is in your partner's name, you may be evicted by your partner, like any other licensee, on reasonable notice followed by a court order.

- Getting an order excluding your partner from the home will not give you any rights which will be binding on third parties such as landlords or building societies; nor will it prevent your excluded partner from removing his household goods.

- As a short-term remedy (usually three months), the court has the power to exclude either one of you from the home, whether or not you are the owner or tenant, if it is fair, just and reasonable to do so and to allow a non-owner to occupy it. The court is required to have regard to:

(a) the parties' conduct;

(b) their respective needs and other financial resources;

(c) the needs of any children; **and**

(d) all the circumstances of the case.

The court then makes such an order as it deems fit in the light of all these considerations.

• If your partner is the owner or tenant of your home, the relationship breaks down and you have a child by your partner living with you, you can apply to the court for an order transferring the property or tenancy either to the child or to you for his benefit (see page 29 for more information).

Bankruptcy

• Even where the home is in your name as well as your partner's, if your partner goes bankrupt, the trustee in bankruptcy will take over your partner's share. If your partner's debts cannot be paid from other assets, the court can order a sale of the property and evict you. The court has the discretion to postpone the sale depending on the circumstances of the case.

• If your partner has, within two years (or five years if he was insolvent at that time), let you have a bigger share of the home than your contribution justifies, on bankruptcy the court can restore the position to what it would have been if your partner had not done so.

Death

- You can succeed your dead partner as the tenant under a local authority tenancy only if you occupied the property as your only or principal home at the time of your partner's death.

- If your partner's tenancy of the home is protected under the Rent Act 1977, the tenancy will devolve according to his Will or intestacy. If the tenancy is a statutory tenancy, you can, on your partner's death, claim a statutory tenancy if you were living with the tenant as husband and wife immediately before his death. It will be necessary to show that a sufficient state of permanence and stability had been reached in the relationship. The mere fact that you were living as a member of the family will not be enough: members of the tenant's family may have stronger claims to succeed than yours.

- If your partner's tenancy is an assured shorthold or assured tenancy for a fixed term, the tenancy will devolve according to his Will or intestacy. If it is an assured periodic tenancy and immediately before death you were occupying the dwelling-house as your only or principal home and the tenant was not a successor to the tenancy, you will be entitled to have the tenancy vested in you. For these purposes, a person who was living with the tenant as husband and wife will be treated as the tenant's spouse.

Married

- By law, every spouse has a right to occupy the matrimonial home so long as the marriage lasts.

This right can be registered and then takes priority over later mortgages or other charges. No-one can be evicted by his spouse except by a court order. Even if one spouse alone owns the home, the court may be willing to make an order evicting him temporarily if it finds it is just and reasonable to do so. It is not essential to show violence but it is necessary to show that the one to be evicted is at fault. The court can also order the evicted owner to make mortgage or rent payments or other outgoings. In doing so, it will have regard in particular to:

(a) the conduct of the spouses;

(b) their needs and financial resources; **and**

(c) the needs of any children.

- The court also has the power to make a permanent property transfer order for the benefit of the other spouse if it is reasonable on his 'needs' (e.g. if there are children to house following a divorce).

Bankruptcy

- If you and your spouse are co-owners of the home and your spouse goes bankrupt, the trustee in bankruptcy will probably not be able to evict you for six months. This is an advantage the co-owning partner does not enjoy.

Death

- You can succeed your dead spouse as the tenant without competing with his other relatives:

(a) under a secure tenancy if you occupied the property as your home at the time of your spouse's death; **or**

(b) under a statutory tenancy under the Rent Act, provided you were residing in the home immediately before his death.

- If your partner's tenancy is an assured shorthold or assured tenancy for a fixed term, the tenancy will devolve according to his Will or intestacy. If it is an assured periodic tenancy and immediately before death you were occupying the dwelling-house as your only or principal home and the tenant was not a successor to the tenancy, you will be entitled to have the tenancy vested in you.

Divorce

- If your spouse is entitled to occupy the matrimonial home under a contractual or local authority tenancy under the Rent Act 1977, the court can transfer that tenancy to you on divorce.

Conclusion

- If you have no legal interest in your home, your right to it is stronger if you are married.

- If your partner has a secure tenancy and may not live long, marriage during the first 12 months of you living together would give you security you would not otherwise have.

Chapter 4

Will your income from your former spouse be affected?

Unmarried

- If you are separated or divorced from your former spouse and are in receipt of maintenance from him but are also being supported by your partner, the court may conclude that you no longer need the maintenance from your former spouse and reduce or cancel it.

Married

- Any order in your favour for maintenance from your former spouse will automatically end once and for all on your remarriage, but you will still be able to pursue any application you made before your remarriage against your former spouse for an order transferring property or the payment of a lump sum. In other words, remarriage brings to an end your right to maintenance from your former spouse but not necessarily your outstanding claim to a capital sum.

Conclusion

- If you receive maintenance from a former spouse, this is an important argument against remarriage. However, if you remarry, you acquire a new set of rights against your new spouse.

Chapter 5

Will you pay less or more tax?

General tax

Men and women, whether they are married or unmarried, are under an obligation to pay tax. Direct tax is calculated and assessed upon each individual separately and each individual is liable to pay what is due.

The rates of tax are the same whether you are living with someone married or unmarried.

Income Tax

Unmarried

Personal allowance

- You will each be entitled to the basic personal tax allowance of £4,745 (2004/05).

Miscellaneous

(a) Payments to a former partner, or to or for the child of unmarried parents, do not attract tax relief.

(b) If you put money in trust for your partner, the income will be taxed as your partner's.

Married

Personal allowance

- Unless one of you was born before 6 April 1935 the position is the same as for unmarried couples, i.e.

you will each be entitled to the basic personal allowance of £4,745 (2004/05).

- Additional allowances are available if either of you were born before 6 April 1935.

Miscellaneous

(a) Payments to a former spouse, or to or for a child of your marriage, do not attract tax relief unless at least one of you was born before 6 April 1935.

(b) If you put money in trust for your spouse, the income will be taxed as yours.

Conclusion

- The different income tax treatment of married and unmarried individuals is being phased out.

- If you put money in trust for your partner, it may make a difference whether you are married or not.

Capital Gains Tax

Unmarried

Transfers between you

- Transfers of property (e.g. land, shares, money and goods) between you will not be exempt from Capital Gains Tax, except up to the free limit every person enjoys of £8,200 (2004/05). If, for example, you transfer to your partner shares worth £100,000 which you purchased some years ago for £60,000, you will have to pay tax at your top Income Tax rate on the gain, subject to your annual exemption and to a relief which increases the longer you have held the shares (called 'taper relief').

Transfers to others/main residence

(a) The same rules apply as in the paragraph above.

(b) The main residence of any person is exempt from Capital Gains Tax upon sale. You can each specify a separate main residence, provided that you do actually live there. So if, for example, you and your partner each own a house and you spend some time in one and some in the other, you can each avoid Capital Gains Tax on your own house when it is sold.

Married

Transfers between you

- Transfers of property between you during marriage will be exempt from Capital Gains Tax provided that you are not separated. The transfer is treated as giving rise to no gain and no loss. Whichever of you subsequently disposes of the property to a third party will be treated as having acquired it at its original cost and will have to pay tax on any gain, subject to a relief which increases the longer the property has been owned by you.

Transfers to others/main residence

(a) You can have only one main residence between you. If you have two houses, one will attract Capital Gains Tax on the profit upon sale. As set out in *Transfers between you* for unmarried couples on page 40, in calculating the liability you each will be entitled to apply for the exemption of £8,200 (2004/05) plus any taper relief.

(b) If you and your spouse separate permanently, the former matrimonial home will cease to be the main residence for at least one of you, although it may remain so for the other. The Inland Revenue have, however, conceded that in this situation Capital Gains Tax may not be payable on the sale or transfer of the house if:

    (i) the transfer or sale takes place within three years of your separation; **and**

    (ii) a formal notification of a new main residence has not been made by the spouse continuing to live in it.

Conclusion

• Transfers between married couples are tax free.

Inheritance Tax

Unmarried

- This is the tax on gifts made during your life and on your estate at death (as well as certain transfers to and out of trusts).

- Inheritance Tax at 40 per cent (2004/05) will be payable on what you receive from your partner's estate, after the first £263,000 (2004/05). 20 per cent will be payable for lifetime transfers into certain kinds of trust.

- Certain transfers are potentially exempt from tax. If a transfer is made between unmarried people and the giver lives longer than seven years after the gift has been made, no Inheritance Tax will be due provided that the giver is completely excluded from any further use or enjoyment of the gift.

Married

- You will not be liable to pay Inheritance Tax on anything you receive from your spouse's estate so long as you are domiciled (have your permanent home) in the UK or you both have a domicile elsewhere (if you are in doubt as to your domicile, which has a technical meaning for tax purposes, speak to your solicitor or accountant). Bearing in mind that liability to Capital Gains Tax is wiped out on death and is generally replaced by Inheritance Tax, this is a valuable exemption for those who are married as the surviving spouse is deemed to have acquired the assets at market value at the date of death. On your death, Inheritance Tax will then be payable on all the assets you leave above £263,000 (2004/05), unless you leave them to a new spouse or to charity.

- A gift of up to £5,000 (2004/05) by your parent(s), £2,500 (2004/05) by your grandparent(s) or £1,000 (2004/05) by one of you to the other is exempt from Inheritance Tax, provided it is a gift made in consideration of you getting married and in the giver's lifetime.

Conclusion

- If your partner may die in the near future leaving you a substantial estate, you will be better off married.

- If you wish to provide for your partner after your death without your estate suffering Inheritance Tax, this is a strong argument in favour of marriage.

Chapter 6

Social security payments: will you win or lose?

The social security system is complex. Basically social security benefits are either contributory or non-contributory. Some of the non-contributory benefits are classed as means-tested in that you can only receive them if you can prove that your income is below a certain level. However, in some cases, even with certain other benefits your entitlement may be affected by other types of income.

Non-means-tested benefits are either contributory or non-contributory:

- **Contributory:** your entitlement depends on the National Insurance contributions you have made while working.

  Included in contributory benefits are: Contribution-based Jobseeker's Allowance, Statutory Sick Pay or Incapacity Benefit, Statutory Maternity Pay or Allowance, Bereavement Payment, Bereavement Allowance, Widowed Parent's Allowance, Category A and Category B Retirement Pension and Graduated Retirement Benefit.

  To receive Statutory Sick Pay or Maternity Pay, you have to have been earning more than the lower earnings limit. It's not necessary for you to have paid a specific number of contributions within a given period as both these benefits are paid by your employer.

- **Non-contributory:** your entitlement depends on your circumstances (including your responsibility for children) or your physical health.

  Included in non-contributory benefits are: Attendance Allowance, Severe Disablement Allowance (abolished for new claims from 6 April 2001), Carer's Allowance (called Invalid Care Allowance prior to April 2003), Disability Living Allowance, Guardian's Allowance, Child Benefit, Industrial Injuries Disablement Benefit and Category D Retirement Pension.

Means-tested benefits include Income Support, Income-based Jobseeker's Allowance, Housing Benefit, Council Tax Benefit, Working Tax Credit, Child Tax Credit and Pension Credit.

An unmarried couple living in one household as husband and wife are treated, for the purpose of means-tested benefits, as if they were married. In this chapter, we shall therefore only consider non-means-tested benefits.

National Insurance contributions

Unmarried

- You are entitled to contributory benefits only if you have made enough appropriate National Insurance contributions previously while working. Each of you will be treated as a single person for the purposes of the contributions you make.

- You will not be able to use your partner's contribution record to claim a retirement pension if your own contributions are insufficient when you reach pensionable age.

- Your contribution record will not even be protected if, for example, you are left with a child to look after and are temporarily unable to work. However, if you have to stay at home to care for a child or a sick or disabled person, you may be entitled to Home Responsibilities Protection (HRP). HRP does not provide contribution credits but reduces the number of qualifying years needed for a full basic pension and other possible benefits you may qualify for in later life.

Married

The position is generally the same as for an unmarried person but there are some differences that have an important effect on your right to claim benefits:

- If you are a woman who was married before 6 April 1977, you had the right from the time of your marriage to pay reduced contributions. If you chose to do so, you cannot claim any contributory benefits in your own right. Entitlement to a retirement pension or widow's benefits on your husband's contributions is not affected, but you will not be entitled to Contribution-based Jobseeker's Allowance, Incapacity Benefit or any other contributory benefit on the basis of reduced rate contributions.

- You can combine or substitute your ex-spouse's record with your own to obtain a retirement pension when you reach pensionable age if you meet certain conditions.

  With respect to Category A Retirement Pensions, you can do so if:

  (a) your contribution record is insufficient to claim the full retirement pension; **and**

(b) you are divorced; **or**

(c) you became a widow or widower before retirement age (60 for a woman, 65 for a man) and you did not remarry before reaching this age.

- You can enjoy this right to substitution even if you are now living with a partner unmarried, but you lose this right if you remarry before you reach pensionable age. If you are a widow, whose widow's or bereavement benefits were suspended before you were 60 because you were cohabiting, you are entitled to have any Category B Retirement Pension to which you may be entitled, paid from your 60th birthday.

- If you become widowed, you may be credited with contributions for any year you were in receipt of Widowed Parent's Allowance to help you qualify for Incapacity Benefit or Contribution-based Jobseeker's Allowance, if you cease to be entitled to Widowed Parent's Allowance for any other reason than remarriage or living with a partner (e.g. returning to work).

Note: A man's rights to rely on his wife's contributions are more limited than his wife's to rely on his.

Non-means-tested benefits

Unmarried

Each of you will be treated as a single person for the purpose of the benefits to which you are entitled.

Adult dependant

By way of exception to the general rule, for certain non-means-tested benefits (e.g. Incapacity Benefit, Severe Disablement Allowance (a benefit which is still in existence but no longer available to new claimants), Carer's Allowance, Category A or C Retirement Pensions and Maternity Allowance), you can get an extra allowance for a partner on top of your own basic benefit if your partner is financially dependent on you **and**:

(a) your partner has the care of a child for whom you are entitled to Child Benefit (or are treated as so entitled because you are living with the child and maintaining him); **and**

(b) your partner is not earning more than a specified amount (the levels allowed are different for each benefit and change each year); **and**

(c) you yourself qualify for one of the non-means-tested benefits which allows you to claim for your partner as an adult dependant (see above); **and**

(d) you and your partner are residing together.

However, do note that if you have resided together and subsequently separate and the child lives with your ex-partner, you may be able to carry on receiving the extra benefit allowance **if**:

(i) your ex-partner agrees to let you claim the Child Benefit for the child (normally Child Benefit is paid to whomever has the child living with him); **and**

(ii) you maintain your ex-partner at least at a rate equal to the increased allowance you are claiming; **and**

(iii) you contribute to the cost of your child at least at the rate of Child Benefit.

Notes:

(a) The person caring for the child can be male or female.

(b) 'Having the care of a child' means performing those duties for a child for which a child needs assistance because it is a child, or exercising that supervision over a child which is one of the needs of childhood. It does not mean exclusive care or more care than that provided by the claimant.

(c) 'Residing together' means living under the same roof with some degree of permanence and continuity. Temporary absences do not count as long as the separation is not likely to be permanent.

Child dependant

The position governing the receipt of Child Benefit is generally the same whether you are living with your partner married or not, or if you are, in fact, alone.

Death

However long you have been living together, and whether or not you have had a child together, a woman will not be entitled to any widow's benefits (which are only available for deaths prior to 9 April 2001) or bereavement benefits (which are only available for deaths on or after 9 April 2001) when her partner dies. (**Note:** From 9 April 2001 widowers are equally entitled to claim for bereavement benefits.)

Married

You may be entitled to the following benefits which you would not get if you were living together unmarried:

Adult dependant women

(a) If you are a married woman with a Category A Retirement Pension, you can claim an extra allowance for your spouse if:

    (i) while you were on Incapacity Benefit you were entitled to an adult dependant's allowance for him immediately before you qualified for your retirement pension; **and**

    (ii) since then, you have not stopped residing with your husband or stopped contributing to his maintenance at a rate at least equal to the amount specified and your husband's earnings have not been higher than the rate specified.

Adult dependant men & women

(a) If you are on Contribution-based Jobseeker's Allowance, Incapacity Benefit, Severe Disability Allowance (a benefit which is still in existence but no longer available to new claimants) or Carer's Allowance, you can claim an extra allowance for your spouse if:

(i) you are not receiving an extra allowance for an adult who cares for your child; **and**

(ii) you are living together; **or**

(iii) you are maintaining your spouse provided that he does not earn more than the specified amount and is not claiming a state benefit of equal or higher value.

(b) If you are a married man drawing your retirement benefit and your spouse is under the age of 60, you can claim an extra allowance for her as a dependant provided that she does not earn more than the specified amount and is not claiming a state benefit of equal or higher value. (**Note:** It is imperative that you provide full disclosure of any benefits received by your dependant when you complete the claim form as this area is a frequent source of overpayments.)

Child dependant

The position is the same as for people living together unmarried.

Category B Retirement Pension (Married Woman's Pension)

(a)   You can claim Category B Retirement Pension on your spouse's contributions if:

  (i)   you and your husband have both reached pensionable age; **and**

  (ii) your husband has satisfied the necessary contribution conditions; **and**

  (iii) your husband is entitled to a Category A Retirement Pension.

(b)   If your husband was receiving an increase of Category A Retirement Pension in respect of you before you received Category B Retirement Pension, this increase is replaced by this pension.

Death

(a)   If your spouse dies on or after 9 April 2001, and he fulfilled the National Insurance contribution conditions (or died as a result of an industrial accident or a disease), you may be entitled to the following:

  (i)   **Bereavement Payment:** a lump sum paid if you are under the age of 60 at the time of your spouse's death. (**Note:** You will not get this payment if you were cohabiting with another person at the time of your spouse's death.) Your entitlement to a Bereavement

Payment is not affected if you remarry after the death of your late spouse.

(ii) **Widowed Parent's Allowance:** a benefit paid if you are a widow who is pregnant or you are a widow(er) who has children with your late spouse or are looking after children whom your late spouse would have been expected to support. (**Note:** You will not get this allowance for any period you cohabit or after you remarry.)

(iii) **Bereavement Allowance:** a benefit paid for up to 52 weeks if you are between the age of 45 and 65 either when your spouse dies or when you cease to be entitled to Widowed Parent's Allowance. (**Note:** You will not get this benefit for any period you cohabit with another person or after you remarry.)

(iv) **Widow's Retirement Pension (Category B Retirement Pension):** a benefit paid to you if you are a widow and your husband dies after you reach the age of 60, or if he dies before you reach 60, when your entitlement to Bereavement Allowance ceases (at the age of 65 at the latest). However, if you remarry before the age of 60, you will lose both your widow's pension and the right to this retirement pension. (**Note:** You will not lose this benefit if you live unmarried with another man as husband and wife.)

(b) If you are a man and your wife dies, you will only get a parallel widower's pension if both you and your wife were over pensionable age when she died. Then, assuming your wife paid enough contributions, you may get the retirement pension for widowers or you may use this pension to make your own up to the basic standard pension. In addition, you may get any additional earnings-related pensions. (**Note:** You will not lose this benefit if you live with a woman unmarried or remarry.)

Conclusion

- For the purpose of claiming benefit in old age or widowhood, there are great advantages in marriage, especially for women and particularly for women who have not been employed.

- If you are not working and paying contributions, and your partner is working, there are advantages in marriage, especially for women.

- If you are widowed or divorced and have not yet reached pensionable age, remember that if your partner has a history of no or low paid work or has little prospect of future work compared with that of your ex-spouse, you may be worse off if you marry him. This is because, from then on, you can claim only on the basis of your second spouse's record.

- If you are in receipt of Widowed Parent's Allowance, there is an argument against marriage. This is because if you remarry you lose it for good, whereas if you merely live with your partner unmarried you will receive it again if and when your relationship terminates.

- If you are a widow under 60 receiving Widow's Retirement Pension, there is an argument against marriage. This is because you will lose both your widow's pension and future entitlements to Widow's Retirement Pension if you remarry.

Note: *Claim Your Cash! How to Collect Your Entitlements* is another book in Lawpack's range which provides further information on all the benefits that you may be entitled to.

Chapter 7

Do you have to support each other financially?

Unmarried

- If there is no binding agreement between you, neither of you are obliged to support the other or each other's children, either while you live together or after you separate so long as you and your partner have no children together. Your position in law is exactly the same as it would be if you were living with another person of the same sex sharing accommodation.

- Where there is a property, interest in that property is broadly determined in accordance with trust principles (for more information, see chapter 2).

- If you make an agreement between you where one of you promises to support the other, the court will enforce it provided that:

    (a) the return for the promise is not immoral;

    (b) it is not merely a domestic arrangement which you never intended to be legally binding;

    (c) it is not an agreement to marry.

- An agreement will be more readily recognised by the court if the main arrangements are summarised in writing and signed by both of you with the help of legal advisers. Like pre-nuptial agreements they are of evidential value; how weighty will depend on the circumstances of the case.

- Many domestic agreements are not enforced because the court decides that they were never intended to be legally binding. An example of such an agreement would be if you were to agree to do the cooking and your partner provide the food, based on the premise that your partner earns more than you do so it seems sensible that you should do the work and your partner pay for it. It would probably be intended that this arrangement would continue for as long as it suits you both and could be altered at any time without either of you being able to sue the other.

- If there is no binding agreement between you but you and your partner have a child together, you can apply to the court for financial support for the child, although not for you.

- If you want a formal promise from your partner but you do not want to make a promise in return, your partner may enter into a covenant under seal (i.e. a deed), for example, to pay you an annual amount for as few or as many years as may be decided. To enforce it, however, you would have to take out proceedings.

Married

- In theory, each of you is liable to maintain the other but whether a court will order either to do so depends on all of the circumstances. Its first consideration would be given to the welfare of any children of the family under the age of 18.

- You can apply to the court for an order for maintenance on the ground that your spouse has failed to provide reasonable maintenance for you. In deciding how much, if anything, should be paid, the court will consider the matters set out on pages

71–72. It is unusual for an order of this kind to be made while the spouses are still living together but in some cases it will be done, for example, if the husband works away from home and goes off without providing enough money to pay the bills.

Conclusion

- Marriage is advantageous if you are likely to need financial support, but it would be a disadvantage for your partner.

- If you are determined not to support your partner, don't get married.

Before marriage

- If, before your marriage, you have made an agreement between you which is intended to govern the situation while you are married, dealing with such matters as maintenance and property, the court will not be bound by it. If either of you have made an application to the court for financial provision, the agreement would be part of the circumstances but no more. How weighty it is will depend on the individual facts of the case.

- Your agreement is likely to have very little effect if you have a child together.

After marriage

- If, after your marriage, you have made an agreement between you containing financial arrangements, any provision purporting to restrict either party's right to apply to the court for an order involving financial arrangements will be void.

- The court can alter the agreement, on application by either of you, if your circumstances have changed or if it does not make proper arrangements for any child of the family.

- If the court does alter the agreement, it will consider all the circumstances in deciding what, if any, order to make.

Conclusion

- The court has the power to alter the effect of what you have agreed.

Chapter 8

What happens when the relationship breaks down?

Note: The various consequences of a relationship breakdown are also dealt with in other chapters of this book. Here we deal only with those general matters not covered elsewhere.

Unmarried

- Either of you can end the relationship and walk out at any time, without notice.

- You are not entitled to maintenance from your partner or any share in his property simply by virtue of your cohabitation and there is no 'palimony' (compensation made by one unmarried partner to the other after separation).

- If you cannot agree over who owns what, you can ask the court to decide. If you own something together and cannot agree that one should pay the other a certain sum for his share, the court will generally order that the item be sold and the proceeds divided as the court decides. The division will be in accordance with strict property rights. The court will generally give one party an opportunity to buy out the other for a specified sum.

- If you have a child by your partner, you can seek periodical payments for the child and an order either for a lump sum or a transfer of property to be made to you for his benefit – see page 21 for more information.

Married

- Although you can leave at any time and live separately from then on, you will remain married in the eyes of the law until the court has granted you a divorce or one of you dies.

Obtaining a divorce

- You may file a petition for divorce based on your domicile or residence. You are 'domiciled' in England & Wales if you regard it as your long-term home, even if you are living abroad. You can be 'resident' in England & Wales if you are actually living here, even if you consider another country to be your long-term home. There are detailed provisions regarding the length of time residence is necessary. Furthermore, certain other European countries have signed a treaty (Brussels II) so that if more than one country has jurisdiction, it becomes a race to file first as it may be better financially to be divorced in one country rather than another. For countries not party to the treaty, it is a matter of arguing which is the most appropriate jurisdiction.

- You may also file a petition for judicial separation under which the court has the same powers as for divorce. The particular features of judicial separation are as follows:

  (a) You do not need to wait a year.

  (b) Except as set out in sub-paragraphs (c) and (d) below, the marriage remains in force so neither party can remarry and when one of you dies, the surviving spouse will be a widow or widower (which may have pension implications when a death occurs).

(c) You are under no obligation to continue cohabiting with your spouse.

(d) If either of you dies intestate (see page 78), the intestacy rules are applied on the assumption that the surviving spouse was already dead. In other words, the separated spouse does not benefit.

(e) The financial remedy on judicial separation may be slightly different to that on divorce, but the court takes the same factors into account (see pages 71–72). However, no pension sharing orders are available.

- You can apply for a divorce after one year of marriage if you can show that your marriage has irretrievably broken down. To prove this, you have to show that:

    (a) your spouse has committed adultery and you find it intolerable to live with him; **or**

    (b) your spouse has deserted you for a continuous period of at least two years; **or**

    (c) your spouse has behaved in such a way that you cannot reasonably be expected to live with him; **or**

    (d) you have both agreed to a divorce after living apart for a continuous period of at least two years; **or**

    (e) you have lived apart for a continuous period of at least five years, unless a divorce would cause your spouse grave financial or any other kind of hardship.

- You cannot get a divorce under sub-paragraphs (d) or (e) above unless the court is satisfied that you are not required to make financial provision for your spouse or that the provision you have made is reasonable and fair or the best that can be made in the circumstances.

- You cannot get a decree absolute of divorce (bringing the marriage to an end and freeing you to remarry) on any ground if the court:

  (a) thinks it should exercise any of its powers regarding any children of the family first;

  (b) is not in a position to do so without giving further consideration to the case; **and**

  (c) directs that the decree is not to be made absolute until it orders otherwise.

Financial provision

- The orders available to you on divorce are interim maintenance (paid as a temporary measure once the divorce petition has been issued pending the fuller hearing), ongoing maintenance (paid to a spouse until either party dies, or the receiving spouse remarries, or a court order changes the arrangements), term maintenance (paid to a spouse for a limited period, or until either party dies, the receiving spouse remarries or a court order), secured maintenance (where a fund or a specific resource (such as property) has to be provided by the payer to stand as security for the maintenance payments), a lump sum, property adjustment orders (i.e. the transfer of property) and pension sharing orders. You can obtain 'clean break' orders if there is enough capital to buy off your maintenance claims.

- In long marriages, if assets exceed needs, the starting point is a 50–50 split on capital, even if one party has been the breadwinner and the other the homemaker. The court will say that each partner has equally 'contributed'.

- When exercising its powers, the court has particular regard to:

  (a) the income, earning capacity, property and other financial resources which each spouse has, or is likely to have, in the foreseeable future including, in the case of earning capacity, any increase in that capacity which it would be reasonable to expect the spouse to take steps to acquire;

  (b) the financial needs, obligations and responsibilities which each spouse has or is likely to have;

  (c) the standard of living enjoyed by the family before the breakdown;

  (d) the age of each spouse and the duration of the marriage;

  (e) any physical or mental disability of either spouse;

  (f) the contributions which each spouse has made, or is likely to make, in the future to the welfare of the family;

(g) the conduct of each spouse if it is such that it would be inequitable to disregard it;

(h) the value to each spouse of any benefit, such as a pension, which by reason of the divorce you will lose the chance of acquiring.

- Although you can keep any lump sum paid to you, an order for periodical payments comes to an end if one of you dies or you remarry or the court makes a further order. The court can vary any periodical payments order upwards or downwards. The mere fact that you live on a long-term basis with a partner will not entitle your spouse to decline to maintain you; this will depend on the circumstances, although the court may reduce the amount.

- You can apply to the court for an order that your spouse should transfer to you all, or any part of, his property, whether acquired before, during or after the marriage or that your spouse pays you a lump sum. The court can also vary any settlement or trust in which you have an interest. This is a form of compulsory redistribution of property between individuals unknown elsewhere in English law. It provides for married people (provided their marriages break down) by granting protection for the poorer at the expense of the richer. A lump sum order can be made even where your spouse does not have property in his possession that can be realised to pay the amount due (e.g. if he is able to borrow it). It is also now possible to ask the court to make a pension sharing order. It can also make orders in relation to death-in-service benefits. This benefit is part of a pension scheme whereby a lump sum is paid to a spouse or beneficiary when the scheme member dies.

- In certain circumstances you have the right to register a notice or restriction over any land or buildings owned by your spouse. This is an important technical step which prevents your spouse from selling or remortgaging the property before the hearing of your claim.

- When the court considers what financial orders to make in your case, it will look at all your circumstances and those of your spouse. It places great emphasis on the need of both parties for a home. It makes its order in the light of the assets and liabilities at the date of the court hearing but resources in the reasonable future are also taken into account. If it is a long marriage and the assets outweigh needs, it is likely the assets will be split equally.

- It is important to note that, except in extreme cases, it does not matter whose fault it is that the marriage broke down.

- If an order for maintenance is made, it may be enforced by various means including:

    (a) an order to take money out of the paying spouse's bank account; **or**

    (b) an order that it be deducted from earnings payable to that spouse by an employer.

- If the order is broken by a spouse who can afford to pay, the court can order imprisonment but not more than once in respect of the same arrears.

- You cannot enforce payment of more than a year's arrears without the leave of the court.

Conclusion

- If you are poorer than your partner, there is a very strong argument for you in favour of marriage; and if you are the richer there is an equally strong argument for you against it. If you are weighing this up, you should think of your future financial position as well as the present.

Chapter 9
What happens when one of you dies?

Unmarried

- If your partner was maintaining you immediately before his death and his Will did not make reasonable financial provision for you, you can apply to the court for an order for provision out of his estate.

'Maintained' means 'received a substantial contribution towards your needs from your partner by way of gifts'. If you cease to be maintained by your partner even a few days before his death, you lose all rights to make a claim.

In deciding what to do the court will consider:

(a) your financial resources and needs;

(b) the financial resources and needs of any other applicant now and in the future;

(c) the financial resources of any beneficiary of the estate now and in the future;

(d) any obligation your partner had towards any applicant or beneficiary;

(e) the size and nature of the estate;

(f) any disability of any applicant or beneficiary;

(g) any other matter including the conduct of the applicant or any other person which is relevant; **and**

(h) the extent to, and basis on, which your partner assumed responsibility for your maintenance and the length of time for which he discharged it.

- If your partner maintained you in his own house for a long time, you may be awarded both the house and some money to live on.

- If your partner dies without making a Will (i.e. intestate), you can make the application as mentioned above, but you will not as of right (i.e. automatically) share in the estate or administer it.

- If your partner dies leaving a Will in your favour, any surviving spouse, dependant ex-spouse and/or dependant children can make a similar claim which is likely to prevail over you (see below).

Married

- If your spouse or ex-spouse has not made reasonable provision for you in his Will, you can apply to the court for an order for financial provision. If your spouse dies, your chances of getting the house are better than those of an unmarried partner and any money you receive will not be restricted to only what you need to live on. The court has to consider what the position would have been if instead of your spouse dying there had been a divorce and takes into account the matters set out on pages 71–72, as well as your age, the duration of the marriage and your contribution to the family (i.e. looking after the home and caring for them).

- If your spouse dies intestate you will be entitled (if you are not judicially separated) to administer his estate and to the following share in it:

(a) If your spouse has not left a child, grandchild, parent, brother or sister, nieces or nephews, or other children: the whole estate.

(b) If your spouse has not left a child or grandchild but a parent, brother or sister or their children: his personal goods, £200,000 and half of the rest of the estate.

(c) If your spouse has left a child or grandchild: his personal goods, £125,000 and a right to the income of half of the rest of the estate for life.

You can, in any case, acquire the matrimonial home as part of your share.

Conclusion

- If your partner is unwilling to make a Will, this would be an argument in favour of marriage.

- Overall, spouses do better than unmarried partners in an application to court if they have not been well provided for on death or if there is no Will.

Chapter 10
Miscellaneous

Bankruptcy

Unmarried

- If you lend money to your partner without security and he goes bankrupt, your claim to repayment will rank with those of the other unsecured creditors.

- Any money payable by your partner to you under an order for your or the children's maintenance can be made the subject of a bankruptcy petition and will be a debt provable in your partner's bankruptcy. If your partner is discharged from bankruptcy, the debt will no longer be recoverable.

- Your right to occupy your home may be lost if your partner becomes bankrupt – see page 32 for further information.

Married

- If you lend money without security to someone who goes bankrupt after marrying you, you can only claim to be repaid after the commercial creditors are paid in full, including interest.

- Sums payable by your spouse to you under a maintenance order are likely to be varied or suspended. Arrears are not a provable debt in bankruptcy but neither will they be discharged with the bankruptcy unless the court so orders. If your spouse is discharged from bankruptcy the debt will still be recoverable.

- If, after a bankruptcy petition has been presented against your spouse, the court orders him (in ignorance of the bankruptcy petition) to transfer any property 'to you', the transfer is likely to be void.

- If your partner transfers any property to you in the five years prior to the making of a bankruptcy order, it is likely that the trustee in bankruptcy will apply to the court to reverse the transfer. This is possible even if the transfer was made pursuant to an order in the family court. Here there is conflict between the bankruptcy court and the family court.

Conclusion

- If you are proposing to lend money to your partner and he is in a weak financial position, this is an argument against marriage. (It would also be an argument for taking out a mortgage or other security to protect your loan.)

Compensation for death

Unmarried

- If your partner dies as a result of the wrongful act of someone else, an action for damages brought by your partner's personal representative against that person can be for your benefit only if you have been living in the same household as your partner for at least two years before his death.

- In assessing your compensation the court will take into account:

(a) the prospect of you marrying someone else;

(b) whether you had a legal right to support from your partner.

- You cannot obtain compensation for bereavement if your partner is killed or, if you are a man, if your child is killed.

Married

- If your spouse dies as a result of the wrongful act of someone else, an action can be brought by your spouse's personal representative for your benefit.

- If you were a married woman, the prospect of you remarrying will not be taken into account in assessing your compensation.

- You can obtain compensation for bereavement of up to £10,000 if your spouse or child is killed by the wrongful act of someone else and if the cause of the action took place after 1 April 2002.

Conclusion

- There is an argument in favour of marriage on this somewhat pessimistic ground which is stronger for women and stronger for men who have a child or for people who have not been living with their partner for as long as two years.

Crime

Unmarried

- If you agree with your partner to commit a criminal offence, you will be guilty of the statutory law offence of conspiracy and liable to a fine or imprisonment.

- If you steal from your partner, you can be prosecuted.

- If a man persistently pesters his partner to have sex with him in a public place, he may be prosecuted for an offence against section 32 of the Sexual Offences Act 1956 and it would be up to the jury to decide if his purpose was immoral. If convicted, he may be sentenced to up to two years' imprisonment.

Married

- If you agree with your spouse alone to commit a criminal offence, you will not be guilty of statutory criminal conspiracy at common law, although you may be liable in damages to someone else.

- If you steal from your spouse, you cannot be prosecuted without the consent of the Director of Public Prosecutions.

- If a man persistently pesters his spouse to have sex with him in a public place, he cannot be guilty of an offence against section 32 of the Sexual Offences Act 1956 as sexual intercourse between spouses cannot be immoral.

Conclusion

- If you are going to steal from your partner, you had better marry him first.

- If you cannot contain your lust until you get home, you had better get married.

Defences

Unmarried

- It is a defence to a criminal charge to show that your partner was present and forced you to commit the crime, provided your partner was threatening to kill or injure you.

Married

- It is currently a defence for a wife to prove that her husband was present and forced her to commit the crime (unless the crime was murder, attempted murder or treason).

Conclusion

- The woman whose partner may force her, without blows or threats of injury, to commit a crime is better off married.

Evidence in court

Unmarried

- You can be compelled to give evidence against your partner.

- You can be compelled to produce a document or answer a question even if it tends to expose your partner to criminal proceedings.

- If you are charged with a crime and on your story in court your partner could give relevant evidence but is not called as a witness on your behalf, the prosecution can comment to the court on the failure to give evidence and this may increase your chance of conviction. There is not the statutory embargo on commenting that there is in relation to spouses.

Married

- You cannot be compelled to give evidence for the prosecution against your spouse, unless the crime:

    (a) involves an assault, injury or threat of injury on him or on someone under 16; **or**

    (b) is a sexual offence against someone under 16; **or**

    (c) is where the spouse is charged with attempting or conspiring to commit, or aiding, abetting, counselling, procuring or inciting the commission of, any of the above offences.

- In a civil case, you cannot generally be compelled to produce any document or answer any question if it would tend to expose your spouse to criminal proceedings. The rule does not apply in cases concerning the recovery or administration of property, information about property (e.g. its location), dealings with property or the execution of a trust. There are also other exceptions:

   (a) Under the intellectual property provisions (such as copyright patents and trademarks), although there is an obligation to disclose information, the evidence produced by the witness is not admissible against either the witness or the spouse in proceedings for an offence under the Theft Act or the Criminal Damage Act.

   (b) In proceedings where the court is hearing any application relating to the care, supervision or protection of a child, no person shall be excused from giving evidence on any matter or answering any question put to him in the course of his giving evidence because it may incriminate him. However, although the witness is compelled to answer questions, he and his spouse receive the protection that the evidence cannot be used against either of them in a criminal case unless they have been charged with perjury, in which case the statements/admissions can be used.

(c)   There are also certain provisions allowing regulatory authorities, liquidators, administrative receivers and inspectors of companies under the Companies Act to require information and documents.

- If you are charged with a crime and on your story in court your spouse could give relevant evidence but is not called as a witness on your behalf, the prosecution cannot comment on it.

Conclusion

- The criminal whose partner knows of the crime is better off married.

- If your partner is going to be sued and has a document revealing your crime, you are better off married.

Employment

Unmarried

- In the vast majority of circumstances, wherever you are employed, if you are living together unmarried and you become pregnant, you cannot lawfully be dismissed on the ground of your pregnancy. There are, however, some exceptions. In one particular case (*Berrisford v Woodwood Schools (Midland Division) (1991) IRLR 247, EAT*), an unmarried individual who was employed as a matron at a

Church of England girls' boarding school was lawfully dismissed when she became pregnant. The dismissal was lawful because it was not due to the pregnancy itself, but because of the adverse example that her pregnancy, coupled with her continuing unmarried status, set to pupils at the school.

Married

- Wherever you are employed, if you become pregnant or the fact of your marriage becomes known, you cannot lawfully be dismissed on these grounds.

Gifts to each other

Unmarried

- Unless you are engaged to be married, if you buy a property and put it in the name of your partner, the law will presume, in the absence of words or circumstances to show that you meant it to be a gift, that you intended that your partner should hold it in trust for you, i.e. for your benefit, and will treat it as such.

- If you put up part of the money to buy a property in your partner's name, the law will presume that your partner has an interest in it.

- If you are engaged to be married but the engagement is broken off, the position is the same as if you were married, except that:

(a) the gift of an engagement ring is presumed to be an absolute gift;

(b) if you make a gift to your partner on the condition that it should be returned if the engagement is terminated, you can still get it back even though you were the one who terminated the engagement.

Married

- The law will presume that if a husband buys property and puts it in the name of his wife, or pays money towards her mortgage, that he intended the payment to be a gift. This will not apply to assets intended at the time of payment to be a continuing provision for both of them, or if his words or the circumstances showed that he did not intend it to be a gift. In the case of assets intended as a continuing provision for both of them, the law will presume that he intended these assets to belong to them both.

- This presumption is much weaker than it used to be and is likely to go altogether. It can be displaced by evidence of the husband's true intention at the time of the payment, but not if the evidence shows that he put the property into his wife's name for an improper purpose, such as to defeat his creditors or to avoid tax.

- The law will presume, if a wife buys a property and puts it in the name of her husband, that she intended that he should hold it in trust for her. This will not apply if her words or the circumstances show that she intended it to be a gift.

Conclusion

- The man who puts property in his partner's name but still cherishes control of it should not marry her.

Life assurance

Unmarried

- You cannot insure your partner's life unless you have a financial interest in it. This is an interest which a court can value, such as an obligation by your partner, under a valid agreement, to maintain you.

- If you insure your own life for the benefit of your partner, the proceeds on your death will form part of your estate and will therefore be subject to Inheritance Tax unless you name your partner as a beneficiary. In this case, your partner will receive the insurance proceeds which will not form part of your estate on death.

Married

- You can insure the life of your spouse.

- If you insure your own life for the benefit of your spouse the proceeds on your death will not form part of your estate if you have nominated your spouse and therefore will not be subject to Inheritance Tax. Even if there isn't a nomination, no tax is payable between spouses.

Conclusion

• If your partner is not bound to support you and you want to insure his life, there is an advantage for you in marriage.

Litigation

Unmarried

• You can sue your partner.

• Any person can usually inspect the claim form or other document starting any court action between you.

• There is generally no bar on reporting the evidence in civil proceedings between you.

Married

• The court has the power to stop certain actions (e.g. negligence) brought by one spouse against the other if it appears that the litigation would not substantially benefit either party. An example might be if you were living together in one household and neither of you were insured against the claim.

- There are special provisions for dealing simply with property disputes between husband and wife. The differences are technical but they are intended to produce a quicker and cheaper determination of your disputes.

- Any person can usually inspect the claim form or other document starting any court action between you.

- No divorce documents held by the court can be disclosed to anyone but the parties and representatives without the court's leave (although a decree absolute is a public document as is the application for decree nisi for a limited period).

Nationality and immigration

Unmarried

Entry clearance & nationality

- If you are present and settled in the UK (or admitted for settlement) and over the age of 18, your unmarried partner over the age of 16 will be granted entry clearance and permission to stay and work in the UK for two years if:

    (a) any previous marriage (or similar relationship) that either you or your partner were in has permanently broken down;

(b) you or your partner have been living together as if you were married for at least two years;

(c) you and your partner intend to live together permanently; **and**

(d) you and your partner have enough money to support and accommodate yourselves and your dependants adequately without help from public funds.

- Nearer the end of your partner's two-year stay, if you and your partner are both still in the relationship and you plan to live together permanently, your partner can apply to remain in the UK permanently.

- Your partner may be granted settlement entry clearance if:

  (a) you and your partner have been living together as if you were married for at least four years; **and**

  (b) you have spent those four years outside the UK; **and**

  (c) you are now returning to the UK to settle here together.

- If you are not married to your partner, your partner can apply for naturalisation after living continuously for five years in the UK. Your partner must have been in the UK on the date five years preceding the date of his application and the number of days he is absent from the UK during this period should not exceed 450 days during the total five years and not more than 90 days in the 12 months preceding the application.

• So far as European Union law is concerned, where a national of any member state of the EU is working as an employee in another member state, his unmarried partner does not have a right to reside with him there.

Children

Different rules apply depending on whether the children are born before, on or after 1 January 1983.

(a) **Pre 1983:** all children who were born in the UK, with the exception of diplomats' children, automatically received British citizenship.

(b) **Post 1983:** your child will be a British citizen by birth in the UK if you or your unmarried partner is, at the time, a British citizen or settled in the UK. If your child is born abroad, he will be a British citizen where either parent is a British citizen otherwise than by descent (i.e. a British citizen who was born, adopted, naturalised or registered in the UK or a qualifying territory).

• Your child will become a British citizen by registration during his childhood if either you or your unmarried partner becomes a British citizen or settles here. Your child may also be entitled to register if he has spent the first ten years of his life in the UK and has not been outside the UK for more than 90 days in respect of any of those years.

Deportation

- If your partner is deported it will make no difference to your right to remain, unless your right to remain is contingent on your partner, and if that is the case you may be deported too. If your partner is a mother of minor children, the children will be deported too.

Married

Entry clearance & nationality

- If you are present and settled in the UK (or admitted for settlement) and over the age of 18, your spouse over the age of 16 will be granted entry clearance and permission to stay and work in the UK for two years if:

  (a) you and your spouse have met and intend to live together permanently as husband and wife; **and**

  (b) you and your spouse have enough money to support and accommodate yourselves and your dependants adequately without help from public funds.

- Nearer the end of your spouse's two-year stay, if you and your spouse are both still in the relationship and you plan to live together permanently, your spouse can apply to stay in the UK permanently.

- Your spouse will be granted settlement entry clearance if:

(a) you and your spouse married four years ago; **and**

(b) you and your spouse spent those four years living together outside the UK; **and**

(c) you are now returning to the UK to settle here together.

- If you are a British citizen, your spouse can apply for naturalisation after only three years in the UK. Your spouse must have been in the UK on the date three years preceding the date of his application and the number of days he is absent from the UK during this period should not exceed 270 during the total three years and not more than 90 in the 12 months preceding the application.

- So far as European Union law is concerned, where a national of any member state of the EU is working as an employee in another member state, his spouse has a right to reside with him there.

Note: Special rules do exist for Commonwealth citizens, but we do not deal with them in this book.

Children

- Different rules apply depending on whether the children are born before, on or after 1 January 1983.

    (a) **Pre 1983:** all children who were born in the UK, with the exception of diplomats' children, automatically received British citizenship. All children born abroad to British citizen fathers (provided the father was married to the child's mother) also automatically qualified for British citizenship.

(b) **Post 1983:** your child will be a British citizen by birth in the UK if you or your spouse is, at the time, a British citizen or settled in the UK. If your child is born abroad, he will be a British citizen where either parent is a British citizen otherwise than by descent (i.e. a British citizen who was born, adopted, naturalised or registered in the UK or a qualifying territory).

- Your child will become a British citizen by registration during his childhood if either you or your spouse becomes a British citizen or settles here. Your child may also be entitled to register if he has spent the first ten years of his life in the UK and has not been outside the UK for more than 90 days in respect of any of those years.

- So far as EU law is concerned, where a national of any member state is working as an employee in another member state, any child of his and his spouse, who is under the age of 21 or dependent on them, may reside with them there. Also, a British National living in another EU country has a right under EU law to bring his spouse and family back with him to the UK.

Deportation

- If your spouse is deported, you are liable to be deported too, unless you have been living apart or you have qualified for settlement in your own right.

Conclusion

- If you are British, your partner is neither British nor settled here and you want your children to be British, marriage is not essential.

- If you are not British and wish to remain here but your partner faces deportation, then marriage should be avoided.

- If you are a national of another member state of the EU coming to take a job here and you would like your partner, who is not a national of an EU member state, to join you, then you should marry your partner.

Partnership

Unmarried

- If you go into partnership with your partner (i.e. run a business in common with a view to profit), the partnership will be governed generally by the law relating to partnerships.

Married

- If you go into partnership with your spouse, or marry your partner, the partnership assets will, if matrimonial proceedings are brought, be part of the property taken into account by the family court. This may mean a considerable redistribution of partnership assets not in accordance with partnership law, although the family court generally treats a business partnership with respect and will only reallocate the assets if the circumstances require.

Conclusion

- If you are unmarried, the partnership assets will be subject to partnership law, whereas if you are married the family court may deal with these assets.

Savings from housekeeping allowance

Unmarried

- If your partner makes you an allowance for the expenses of your joint home, the money or any property acquired with it will, in the absence of agreement between you to the contrary, be treated as your partner's.

Married

- If the husband makes his wife any allowance for the expenses of the matrimonial home, the money or any property acquired with it will, in the absence of agreement between them to the contrary, be treated as belonging to them both.

Conclusion

- The frugal woman, whose partner is generous with his housekeeping allowance, would be better off getting married.

Titles

Unmarried

- If your partner is knighted or made a Dame or a peer, your title remains unaltered and if the title is hereditary your child will not succeed to it.

Married

- If your husband is knighted (Sir X) or made a peer (Lord X), you are entitled to describe yourself as Lady X, and if the title is hereditary your child will succeed to it.

Conclusion

- If you want a title like your partner, you are better off married.

Violence

Married and unmarried

- You can apply to the court for a non-molestation order, restraining the other party from assaulting, intimidating, harassing or threatening to use violence against you and/or any children of the family.

- You can also apply to the court for an occupation order excluding the other party from the property. A Power of Arrest will be attached to the order. It is difficult to obtain an occupation order in the absence of violence.

- These types of orders generally last for about six months unless they are renewed by the court.

Wills

Unmarried

- Your Will is unaffected.

Married

- Your Will is revoked by marriage unless it was made in anticipation of marriage to your spouse.

- On divorce, any provision in your Will making your spouse an executor or beneficiary will cease to be effective.

Conclusion

- If you marry, you are likely to need a new Will, unless you have made one in contemplation of marriage.

Conclusion

So, in conclusion, is marriage the better buy? Apart from particular cases to which we draw attention in this book, the answer is: it depends.

In general, a first marriage is the better buy for most people provided the relationship does not break down. Second or further marriages may not be the better buy as you may lose various advantages from your previous marriage, such as the right to fall back on maintenance from your ex-spouse.

If the relationship does break down, marriage is the better buy for the poorer of you, for the father who wants to be on an equal footing with the mother of his child or if your partner dies; but marriage is not the better buy for the richer of you or for the person who does not want any obligation towards his partner's child by someone else. Indeed, even if the relationship does not break down, the survivor after the other's death is better off as a spouse than a partner.

Final note

This book is intended as a summary. If you are considering getting married for one of the reasons detailed in this book, you would be wise to consult a solicitor initially and possibly an accountant afterwards in order to obtain detailed advice.

Appendix

Hague & European Convention countries

Countries in which the Hague and European Conventions are in force with the UK as at 1 October 2003

Argentina	Hague	
Australia	Hague	
Austria	Hague	European
Bahamas	Hague	
Belarus	Hague	
Belgium	Hague	European
Belize	Hague	
Bosnia & Herzegovina	Hague	
Bulgaria		European
Burkina Faso	Hague	
Canada (most states)	Hague	
Chile	Hague	
Colombia	Hague	
Croatia	Hague	
Cyprus (Southern)	Hague	European
Czech Republic	Hague	European
Denmark	Hague	European
Ecuador	Hague	
Estonia	Hague	European
Fiji	Hague	
Finland	Hague	European
France	Hague	European
Georgia	Hague	
Germany	Hague	European
Greece	Hague	European
Honduras	Hague	
Hong Kong	Hague	
Hungary	Hague	
Iceland	Hague	European
Ireland	Hague	European

Israel	Hague	
Italy	Hague	European
Latvia	Hague	European
Liechtenstein		European
Lithuania		European
Luxembourg	Hague	European
Macao	Hague	
Macedonia	Hague	European
Malta	Hague	European
Mauritius	Hague	
Mexico	Hague	
Monaco	Hague	
Netherlands	Hague	European
New Zealand	Hague	
Norway	Hague	European
Panama	Hague	
Peru	Hague	
Poland	Hague	European
Portugal	Hague	European
Romania	Hague	
Serbia & Montenegro	Hague	European
Slovakia	Hague	European
Slovenia	Hague	
South Africa	Hague	
Spain	Hague	European
St Kitts & Nevis	Hague	
Sweden	Hague	European
Switzerland	Hague	European
Turkey	Hague	European
Uruguay	Hague	
USA	Hague	
Uzbekistan	Hague	
Venezuela	Hague	
Zimbabwe	Hague	

Index

MORE BOOKS AVAILABLE FROM LAWPACK

The Buy-to-Let Bible

Low mortgage rates and under-performance by traditional savings and investment products means that property has never looked a better way to invest for the future. Author Ajay Ahuja divulges the practical and financial techniques that have made him a millionaire. It covers finding the right property, the right mortgage lender, the right tenant, legal issues and tax.

Code B437 | ISBN 1 904053 36 X | Paperback | 245 × 199mm | 160pp | £11.99 | 2nd edition

Buying Bargains at Property Auctions

Every week, hundreds of commercial and residential properties are sold at auction in Britain, often at bargain prices, with owner-occupiers accounting for a growing proportion of buyers. In this bestselling guide, author and property auctioneer Howard Gooddie spells out how straightforward the auction route can be and divulges the tips and practices of this relatively unknown world.

Code B426 | ISBN 1 904053 37 8 | Paperback | 245 × 199mm | 176pp | £11.99 | 2nd edition

Residential Lettings

Are you thinking of letting a flat or a house? This guide steers anyone who intends - or already is - letting property through the legal and practical issues involved. It provides all the up-to-date information and tips that a would-be landlord needs. It will also alert existing landlords to the points of good practice that make a letting successful, and the legal obligations that they may not be aware of.

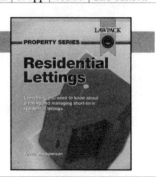

Code B422 | ISBN 1 904053 34 3 | Paperback | 245 × 199mm | 104pp | £11.99 | 3rd edition

To order, visit www.lawpack.co.uk or call 020 7394 4040

MORE BOOKS AVAILABLE FROM LAWPACK

Employment Law

Whether you are an employer or an employee, you have ever-increasing rights and duties in the workplace. This bestselling guide, by specialist solicitor Melanie Slocombe, is a comprehensive source of up-to-date knowledge on hiring, wages, employment contracts, family-friendly rights, discrimination, termination and other important issues. It puts at your fingertips the important legal points that all employers and employees should know about.

Code B408 | ISBN 1 904053 30 0 | Paperback | 240 × 167mm | 192pp | £11.99 | 6th edition

Separation & Divorce

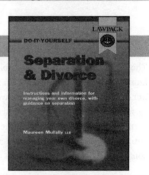

Separation and divorce do not have to be very costly and difficult. This guide gives you the instructions and information you need to manage your own divorce, without the expense of a solicitor. It explains the legal and financial issues involved, and takes you step-by-step from the petition to the final decree. For use in England & Wales.

Code B445 | ISBN 1 904053 32 7 | Paperback | 240 × 167mm | 216pp | £11.99 | 1st edition

Wills, Power of Attorney & Probate

This guide combines three closely related areas of law; the common theme is the management of personal property and legal affairs. In a Will, you set out whom is to inherit your 'estate'; a power of attorney authorises another to act on your behalf with full legal authority; and via probate (or 'Confirmation' in Scotland), executors gain authority to administer your Will.

Code B407 | ISBN 1 904053 33 5 | Paperback | 240 × 167mm | 248pp | £11.99 | 1st edition

To order, visit **www.lawpack.co.uk** or call **020 7394 4040**

MORE BOOKS AVAILABLE FROM LAWPACK

Affordable Law

Whenever anyone considers visiting a lawyer often the first thought is how much will it cost. It has been three years since the Government dismantled Legal Aid; it was anticipated that 'No win, no fee' agreements would - more or less - fill the gap. But this has been met with confusion and misunderstanding, added to which have been the recent consumer scares. This handbook provides guidance on the different means of funding the most common legal actions.

Code B443 | ISBN 1 904053 44 0 | Paperback | A5 | 192pp | £7.99 | 1st edition

Claim Your Cash!

Thousands of people may be eligible for financial help and not know it - this handbook tells them what they could be missing out on. Three quarters of all taxpayers pay more than they need to. Millions of pounds go unclaimed in welfare benefits each year. This handbook sets out all the main payments you may be entitled to, describing how you go about claiming and giving some useful tips to ensure the best chance of success.

Code B434 | ISBN 1 904053 51 3 | Paperback | A5 | 240pp | £7.99 | 2nd edition

Tax Answers at a Glance

We all need to have a hold of the array of taxes now levied by the Government. Compiled by award-winning tax experts and presented in question-and-answer format, this handbook provides a useful and digestible summary of Income Tax, VAT, capital gains, inheritance, pensions, self-employment, partnerships, land and property, trusts and estates, Corporation Tax, Stamp Duty and more.

Code B425 | ISBN 1 904053 62 9 | Paperback | A5 | 208pp | £7.99 | 4th edition

To order, visit **www.lawpack.co.uk** or call **020 7394 4040**

MORE BOOKS AVAILABLE FROM LAWPACK

Health and Safety at Work Essentials

Every workplace has to comply with an extensive range of health and safety rules and regulations. With more legal claims being made daily, the price for failing to comply, whether through fines or claims by employees, can be high. This is a handy, 'one-stop' handbook for anyone responsible for health and safety issues in the workplace. It sets out the background legal basics and provides succinct, practical advice on what measures to take.

Code B435 | ISBN 1 904053 52 1 | Paperback | A5 | 176pp | £7.99 | 3rd edition

Home & Family Solicitor

The essential do-it-yourself legal resource for every home. From taking action against a noisy neighbour to drawing up a live-in nanny's employment contract, this book of forms will provide you with the ideal, ready-to-use legal letter or agreement. Covers: credit and finance, employment, goods, services and utilities, insurance, personal and family matters, lettings and property, and local environment.

Code B418 | ISBN 1 902646 30 4 | Paperback | A4 | 232pp | £19.99 | 3rd edition

301 Legal Forms, Letters & Agreements

Our best-selling form book now in its seventh edition. It is packed with forms, letters and agreements for legal protection in virtually every situation. It provides a complete do-it-yourself library of 301 ready-to-use legal documents, for business or personal use. Areas covered include loans and borrowing, buying and selling, employment, transfers and assignments and residential tenancy.

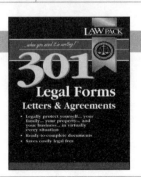

Code B402 | ISBN 1 902646 72 X | Paperback | A4 | 384pp | £19.99 | 7th edition

To order, visit **www.lawpack.co.uk** or call **020 7394 4040**